# The Tao

## of Women

Pamela K. Metz
Jacqueline L. Tobin

# The
# Tao
## of Women

## Pamela K. Metz
## Jacqueline L. Tobin

Humanics Trade
PO Box 7400
Atlanta, GA 30357

Humanics Trade
PO Box 7400
Atlanta, GA 30357

PRINTED IN THE UNITED STATES OF AMERICA

Metz, Pamela, 1940- .
    The Tao of women/Pamela Metz and Jacqueline Tobin.
        p.   cm.
    Includes bibliographical references.
        ISBN 0-89334-237-8 (trade paper). -- ISBN 0-89334-245-9 (lib. bind).
        1. Women   2. Philosophy   3. Tao I.  Tobin, Jacqueline, 1950-
    II.  Title.

305.4--dc20
                                                                    95-14162
                                                                         CIP

Cover and text design by Susan Chamberlain

# Acknowledgments

We wish to thank our families, friends, colleagues, students, teachers, and especially all of the women who have contributed directly and indirectly to *The Tao of Women*. We acknowledge the synchronicity in discovering the *Nu Shu* and wish to thank Norma Libman for writing about it initially; and Su Chien-ling at The Awakening Foundation for connecting us to our Nu Shu translator, Shi-huei Cheng. We have been privileged to work with all of you.

Pamela would like to thank Gary Wilson and Robin Hall of Humanics Limited for continuing the tradition of publishing the Tao books, Charlene Byers for unfailing friendship, and all of the women and men who helped her on this path.

Jacqueline would like to thank her husband, Stewart, for supporting her endeavors with "a room of her own;" her children, Alex and Jasmine, who have shown her real connections; her mother who left her with a legacy to pass on; and her sisters, B.J. and Debra, who believed in her.

# Contents

Introduction . . . . . . . . . . . . . . . . . . . . . . . . . . . .1

1   Emergence . . . . . . . . . . . . . . . . . . . . . . . . . .4

2   Women's Work . . . . . . . . . . . . . . . . . . . . . .6

3   Knowing Woman . . . . . . . . . . . . . . . . . .8

4   Containers . . . . . . . . . . . . . . . . . . . . . .10

5   Balance . . . . . . . . . . . . . . . . . . . . . . . . .12

6   Womb . . . . . . . . . . . . . . . . . . . . . . . . . .14

7   Connection . . . . . . . . . . . . . . . . . . . . .16

8   Fluid . . . . . . . . . . . . . . . . . . . . . . . . . . .18

9   Fullness . . . . . . . . . . . . . . . . . . . . . . . .20

10  Birthing . . . . . . . . . . . . . . . . . . . . . . . .22

11  Between the Lines . . . . . . . . . . . . . . . . .24

12  Intuition . . . . . . . . . . . . . . . . . . . . . . . .26

13  Her Self/Herself . . . . . . . . . . . . . . . . . .28

14  Wisdom . . . . . . . . . . . . . . . . . . . . . . . .30

15  Wise Women . . . . . . . . . . . . . . . . . . . .32

16  Cycles . . . . . . . . . . . . . . . . . . . . . . . . .34

17  Midwifery . . . . . . . . . . . . . . . . . . . . . .36

18  Forgetting/Remembering . . . . . . . . . . . .38

19  Flowing From the Center of the Web . . . . . . . . .40

20  Solitary . . . . . . . . . . . . . . . . . . . . . . . .42

21  Reflection . . . . . . . . . . . . . . . . . . . . . . . . . . .44

22  Mirroring . . . . . . . . . . . . . . . . . . . . . . . . . . . .46

23  Embodiment . . . . . . . . . . . . . . . . . . . . . . . . .48

24  Grounded . . . . . . . . . . . . . . . . . . . . . . . . . . .50

25  Source . . . . . . . . . . . . . . . . . . . . . . . . . . . . . .52

26  Home . . . . . . . . . . . . . . . . . . . . . . . . . . . . . . .54

27  Journeying . . . . . . . . . . . . . . . . . . . . . . . . . .56

28  Opposites . . . . . . . . . . . . . . . . . . . . . . . . . . .58

29  Seasons . . . . . . . . . . . . . . . . . . . . . . . . . . . .60

30  Courage . . . . . . . . . . . . . . . . . . . . . . . . . . . .62

31  Silence . . . . . . . . . . . . . . . . . . . . . . . . . . . . .64

32  Women and Men: The Tao . . . . . . . . . . . . . . . .66

33  Know Thyself . . . . . . . . . . . . . . . . . . . . . . . . .68

34  Women's Mysteries . . . . . . . . . . . . . . . . . . . .70

35  Walking the Sacred Way . . . . . . . . . . . . . . . .72

36  The Way of Women . . . . . . . . . . . . . . . . . . . .74

37  Transformation . . . . . . . . . . . . . . . . . . . . . . .76

38  Scripts . . . . . . . . . . . . . . . . . . . . . . . . . . . . . .78

39  Fragments of the Whole . . . . . . . . . . . . . . . . .80

40  Return . . . . . . . . . . . . . . . . . . . . . . . . . . . . . .82

41  Path . . . . . . . . . . . . . . . . . . . . . . . . . . . . . . . .84

42  Community of One . . . . . . . . . . . . . . . . . . . . . . . .86

43  Gentle . . . . . . . . . . . . . . . . . . . . . . . . . . . . . . . .88

44  Contentment  . . . . . . . . . . . . . . . . . . . . . . . . . . .90

45  Doing the Work of the Tao  . . . . . . . . . . . . . . . .92

46  Fear . . . . . . . . . . . . . . . . . . . . . . . . . . . . . . . . . .94

47  Trusting Emotions  . . . . . . . . . . . . . . . . . . . . . .96

48  Rituals . . . . . . . . . . . . . . . . . . . . . . . . . . . . . . . .98

49  Family . . . . . . . . . . . . . . . . . . . . . . . . . . . . . . . .100

50  Rhythms of Living  . . . . . . . . . . . . . . . . . . . . . .102

51  Mother Nature  . . . . . . . . . . . . . . . . . . . . . . . . .104

52  Finding Your Way . . . . . . . . . . . . . . . . . . . . . . .106

53  Staying on the Path When the Way is Lost  . . . .108

54  Women Who Have Gone Before . . . . . . . . . . . . .110

55  Natural Immunity . . . . . . . . . . . . . . . . . . . . . . .112

56  Creative Spirit  . . . . . . . . . . . . . . . . . . . . . . . . .114

57  Ordinary to Heroic . . . . . . . . . . . . . . . . . . . . . .116

58  Giving Yourself Away . . . . . . . . . . . . . . . . . . . .118

59  Nurturing . . . . . . . . . . . . . . . . . . . . . . . . . . . . .120

60  Incubation . . . . . . . . . . . . . . . . . . . . . . . . . . . .122

61  Receptive  . . . . . . . . . . . . . . . . . . . . . . . . . . . .124

62  Telling the Stories  . . . . . . . . . . . . . . . . . . . . . .126

63  Discrimination: Sorting Seeds . . . . . . . . . . . . . .128

64  Beginnings Without Ends  . . . . . . . . . . . . . . . . .130

65 Simple Patterns . . . . . . . . . . . . . . . . . . . . . . . . .132

66 Collaborating . . . . . . . . . . . . . . . . . . . . . . . . .134

67 Gifts to Herself . . . . . . . . . . . . . . . . . . . . . . . .136

68 Playful Spirit . . . . . . . . . . . . . . . . . . . . . . . . . .138

69 Patience . . . . . . . . . . . . . . . . . . . . . . . . . . . . .140

70 Spirituality . . . . . . . . . . . . . . . . . . . . . . . . . . .142

71 Healing . . . . . . . . . . . . . . . . . . . . . . . . . . . . . .144

72 Modeling . . . . . . . . . . . . . . . . . . . . . . . . . . . . .146

73 Web of the World . . . . . . . . . . . . . . . . . . . . . . .148

74 Change . . . . . . . . . . . . . . . . . . . . . . . . . . . . . .150

75 Cutting the Cord . . . . . . . . . . . . . . . . . . . . . . . .152

76 Subtleties . . . . . . . . . . . . . . . . . . . . . . . . . . . .154

77 Stability . . . . . . . . . . . . . . . . . . . . . . . . . . . . .156

78 Power of the Feminine . . . . . . . . . . . . . . . . . . .158

79 Self-Responsibility . . . . . . . . . . . . . . . . . . . . . .160

80 Setting Priorities: Saying No . . . . . . . . . . . . . . .162

81 Knowing Women . . . . . . . . . . . . . . . . . . . . . . .164

Bibliography . . . . . . . . . . . . . . . . . . . . . . . . . . . . .167

About the Authors . . . . . . . . . . . . . . . . . . . . . . . . .175

About the Artists . . . . . . . . . . . . . . . . . . . . . . . . . .175

Reflections . . . . . . . . . . . . . . . . . . . . . . . . . . . . . .176

# The

# Tao

## of Women

# Introduction

The Tao of Women, inspired by Lao Tzu's Tao Te Ching, links ancient Taoist philosophy with feminine wisdom. Shortly before his death, Lao Tzu was persuaded by his followers to record his life's teachings in the form of 81 chapters or verses. His Tao Te Ching, "Book of the Way," has been a source of philosophical reflections for millions. We use the same format here in our desire to recapture and present the wisdom generated from centuries of women's lives with the hope that this wisdom will not be lost. The Tao of Women means "The Way of Women." We knew intuitively that if we were to remain still and listen carefully, we would be guided by the voices and messages of our female ancestors.

Women's stories have not been brought to light and examined through publication, or even spoken about until relatively recently. These stories are hidden in the quilts we sew, the baskets we weave, the pottery we design, the songs we sing, the poems we create, and the families we raise – the messages of entire lives encoded in the female traditions. All women share the power to create; we are the origins and endless possibilities of life. In several brief, poignant meditations, we attempt to capture this power and explore the many perspectives and roles of women throughout the ages.

Countless generations of women have gone before us. Tales of the remarkable lives of ordinary women have either been lost to time or forgotten altogether. We recognize that women no longer gather at the well; mothers and daughters no longer sit side by side; grandmothers are left with no one to teach. The primary lines of women's communication, already delicate and tenuous, become more and more removed from our daily lives.

In the midst of writing The Tao of Women, an article by Ms. Norma Libman appeared in our local newspaper, reporting the recent discovery of a 1000 year old secret language once used by women in China. This secret language, called Nu Shu, ("women's script"), was developed as a means of communication in a society where only men were publicly allowed to read or write. In stark, simple characters, women communicated despite their oppressions. By design, this language is small and simple. It is easily deciphered by the trained eye, but virtually insignificant to those who do not know what to look for. Nu Shu would be sketched between the vertical lines of traditional Chinese writing, or sewed into handkerchiefs, fans, and napkins sent as unassuming gifts. We have been told only a few elderly Chinese women still use Nu Shu in their personal lives, having been taught the skill by their mothers and grandmothers. We immediately knew that this secret form of communication had to be preserved and cherished.

Nu Shu first came to public attention in 1950 in the mountainous area of Hunan, China. A woman trying to find her childhood home went to a police station with her address written on a slip of paper, written in the Nu Shu script. No one could understand the language, no one there had ever seen it before. It was not until 1982 that this secret language was successfully collected and translated.

In Hunan Buddhist tradition, all possessions are burned when one dies, so many of the original artifacts containing the language were destroyed. Hoping to preserve this cultural heritage before the last known writer died, ethnologist Hung Che-ping went to Hunan. There she gathered, studied, and translated all the works of Nu Shu she could recover. Were it not for her diligence and curiosity, a wealth of handwritten Nu Shu songs, poems, stories, letters, and autobiographies would have been irretrievably lost.

Ms. Shi-huei Cheng, an editor, translator, and board member of the Chinese feminist organization, The Awakening Foundation, translated the titles of each of the 81 chapters found here in The Tao of Women. These are the only examples of Nu Shu published in the English language. She has conducted extensive fieldwork in Hunan with the handful of women who still use Nu Shu, and has edited some of the original Nu Shu manuscripts and their Mandarin translations. She was recommended to us by Su Chien-ling, the Vice Chairwoman of The Awakening Foundation, and we greatly appreciate all of their help.

We feel very honored to have the chapter headings of this book illustrated with the Nu Shu translations. How appropriate for the ancient and mystical Tao to be in partnership with the mysterious female language in a book that presents a contemporary telling of the ways of women. The traditional Chinese characters have been added not only to show the stark disparity between the two forms of communication, but to exhibit how the original placement of Nu Shu might have appeared. We hope to achieve a balance of male

2

and female, the masculine and the feminine. Women have survived by understanding balance and wholeness: being female and giving birth to males, being gentle to overcome obstacles, and stepping back to get ahead. We celebrate and embrace this female wisdom.

Within each chapter there is a space for you to record your own reflections. In an effort to revitalize the tradition of passing along women's histories, we encourage you to use this book as a journal of your thoughts, theories, questions, and stories. It has been a long time since women have connected and communicated deeply, since women have spoken to one another about what is means to be a woman. There is an address provided at the end of the book for you to send us your favorite reflection. It could be a poem, a drawing, a story, or advice, any personal reflection you choose. These chapters are our teachings for living life as a woman, the wisdom we want our daughters to have. What lessons would you like to pass on? What are the lessons that connect us all as women that you want to share?

Although women have survived throughout history by living in silence, their power can be heard by those who listen. Women in all cultures, without their own voice or language, often times without the ability to read or write, have always found ways to communicate. *The Tao of Women* is a modern day version of the *Nu Shu* language. Read between these lines and you will find the eternal language of women. It remains a secret only to those who do not try or want to understand. With these verses and translations, we break the silence, claim our wisdom as women, and know that which connects us all. When the silence is broken and the code deciphered, we discover the thread of female tradition that connects us as women. This thread can serve as a guide through the labyrinth of life's unfolding passages, guiding us along the path walked by so many before us. *The Tao of Women* is woven with this thread.

Speak the verses aloud to yourselves and to each other. Hear the voices of our grandmothers and their grandmothers in the silences between the words. Visualize our connections to each other over time and space and culture. Remember the women who came before and the daughters who follow.

*The Tao of Women* is your legacy. Pass it on.

# Reflections

現

Emergence

# 1 Emergence

From the Tao emerge the stories connecting all women.

The threads have lain hidden for thousands of years.

Paths have been worn by the feet of the ones who have gone before.

Stories were silenced. Lives forgotten.

Now, the shattering of silence; a chorus rising. The women are speaking.

Emergence.

Reflections

Women's Work

# 2 Women's Work

She dares to create the extraordinary from the ordinary.

She takes scraps, pieces, and leftovers, and fashions quilts, baskets, pies, and families.

Having and not having provide the tension for creation.

She dares to create without doing, weave without thread, and sing through the silence.

When women's work is done, she lets it go. In this way, it can continue without her.

Extraordinary.

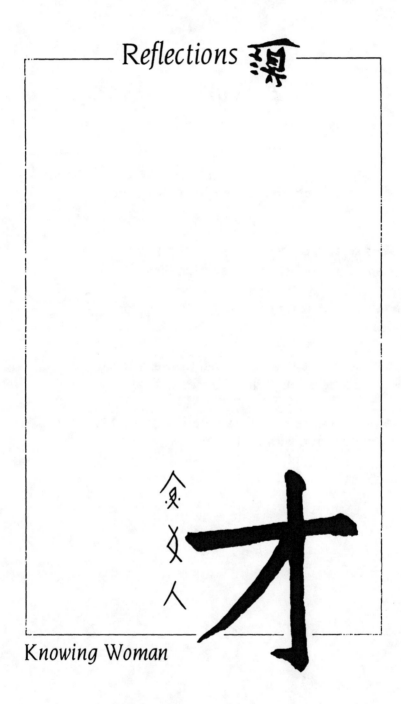

Knowing Woman

# 3 Knowing Woman

She is a knowing woman who goes about her business and lets others do the same. Everything gets done when we get out of each other's way.

She has learned what is important and takes time to visit her neighbor. She celebrates famous women and honors all others by rejoicing in their connections.

She is sure of her place in the world and creates room for others. Her lifetime of experiences have brought her here.

# Reflections 溟

Containers

10

# 4  Containers

She contains that which nourishes the world.

Pouring freely, the wise woman first quenches her own thirst.

Balance

# 5  Balance

The wise woman is like a mother; she brings both good and bad into the world. The wise woman is neutral; she opens her arms to all people.

The Tao is like the wise woman; it is free of bias and able to stay balanced. The more she gives away, the more she has. The more talk there is about her, the less she is understood.

Stay centered; stay balanced.

Womb

# 6 Womb

The wise woman remembers her origins. She
returns often for self-renewal and re-birth.

For the children of the world, Mother Earth offers
a safe place to explore, a source of nourishment,
and possibility for growth.

The wise woman guards the natural order of
creation.

Connection

16

# 7 Connection

The wise woman maintains her connection to all things by letting go.

The boy child clinging to the breast does not grow to be a man.

Let go.

The girl child living out her mother's dreams does not grow to be a woman.

Let go.

The web that holds the spider cannot be seen. Yet, it maintains its connection for freedom and safety.

Let go.

Fluid

18

# 8  Fluid  )|(

The wise woman can take the shape of her
space but does not lose her form. It is not
essential to her nature to stay inside the lines.

She does not give up that which holds her
together; therefore, she is free.

Reflections

Fullness

20

# 9 Fullness

The full cup can receive no more. The empty cup waits to be filled.

The wise woman's cup is always half full, ready to receive and ready to give.

# Reflections

Birthing

22

# 10 Birthing

Can you give birth and still let go? Can you
nourish others and continue to take care of
yourself?

Can you show others the way without losing your
own? Can you provide safety yet dare to risk the
unknown?

Can you calm the fears of children while embracing
your own?

Everything you touch changes. You change
everything you touch. The process is creation.

# Reflections 源

Between the Lines 閒

24

# 11 Between the Lines

The space between the lines creates the picture. Shaping meaning in our lives, the figure and the background are reversed. It is not an illusion.

Emptiness is full; fullness leaves no space for emptiness.

Outside the margins lies her wilderness, her place to be with other women, remembering sacred spaces that exist between the lines for those who search.

Emptiness is full. Between the lines holds mystery.

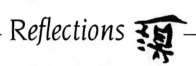

Intuition

26

# 12 Intuition

Her power lies in the direct perception of life without naming.

Intuition: intelligence beyond words; survival skills.

Trust your intelligence. Respond to the heart of the matter.

她

*Her Self/Herself*

28

# 13  Her Self/Herself

To climb a mountain or descend it, to succeed or to fail, the process is the same. One step at a time. Which is more difficult?

Maintaining her connections to the earth, she is connected to her self. Every step the wise woman takes is sacred ground.

Wisdom

# 14 Wisdom

If you seek wisdom, dare to cross boundaries and step out of line. Sit beside the women and men doing the work by hand. Participate in life.

Listen to the teachers and speak with other students. Close the books. Knowledge is not wisdom.

# Reflections

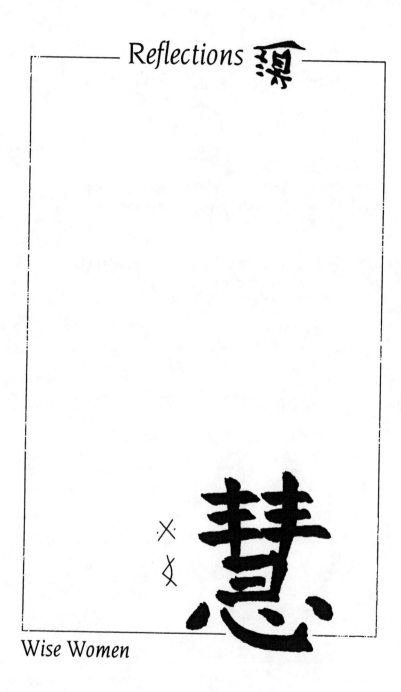

Wise Women

32

# 15  Wise Women

Wise women walk among us in the roles of sister, daughter, lover, mother, friend. They do what needs to be done and move on without recognition.

Appearances are deceptive. How can you see before you are ready? The wise woman does not seek recognition, lest she be misunderstood.

The wise woman knows how to survive. She appears in many forms.

If you wish to know her, begin now. Walk city streets. Climb mountains. Read books. Talk with virgins. Look in your mirror. She is everywhere.

Cycles

# 16 Cycles

There must be separation before one can return.
There must be winter before there can be spring.

Every seed needs a time for growth; every woman
needs a time for herself.

The moon creates the tides. A woman in touch
with her own nature welcomes the ebb and flow of
life.

Midwifery

# 17 Midwifery

In the birthing process, the wise woman enables the mother to give birth by herself.

A midwife removes obstructions, creates safety, and stays out of the way.

After the birth, the mother takes pride in the process of natural childbirth.

"I did it myself," she says, as the midwife slips away.

# Reflections 渠

Forgetting/Remembering

38

# 18 Forgetting/Remembering

When the ways of women are forgotten, only the stories of men are heard.

Without the stories of women, only male heroes are born.

When the language spoken can be understood by only half the community, the wisdom of the ages is lost.

Reinventing the wheel every generation should not be necessary.

Flowing From the
Center of the Web

40

# 19  Flowing From the Center
## of the Web

Working from her center, the wise woman moves
outward. She does what has to be done.

Throw away the "shoulds" and the work gets done.
Throw away the roles and everyone can join in.

Working from her center, the wise woman
encounters little resistance.

Life flows.

Reflections

*Solitary*

42

# 20 Solitary

When you stop worrying, your problems disappear. Does it really matter if you win or lose? Is it really important to follow the crowd and imitate others?

Even though others give up their identity to fit into the molds, I don't care. I stand with the children in their innocence.

Even though others have possessions, I remain empty and without a home. My mind remains open.

Other women shine; I am dull. Other women are cutting; I am without edge. Other women live with purpose; I am still searching.

I drift like snow in a storm. I seem aimless and without direction.

Yet, in my difference, I am solid in my connection to the earth.

Reflection

# 21 Reflection

The moon is not tamed because it is named. The tides still come and go as always.

Dark, unfathomable, and mysterious, the power of reflection is in direct proportion to the power of the Source.

One cannot exist without the other. Obstacles obstruct.

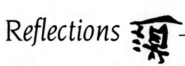

*Mirroring*

# 22 Mirroring

Shattering the mirror does not eliminate the image. Every piece contains the whole. Every seed contains the kernel for greatness. The wise woman reflects the potential in all matter.

Embodiment

48

# 23 Embodiment

Trust your instincts. They embody your
authentic responses to your surroundings.

When life provides pain, embrace your grief and
sadness. When life provides joy, celebrate your
happiness.

The wise woman embodies this moment's grace,
then gives herself over to the next.

Grounded

50

# 24 Grounded

Stretching herself too thin, she breaks her connections. Staying too busy, she has no time. Doing for others, she neglects herself.

Defining herself only through others, she loses her own definition.

The wise woman waters her own garden first.

# Reflections

Source

52

# 25 Source

The deer searches for the source of its own musk, the woman for the source of her own power. When she attributes it to others, she empowers them. When she stops her search, she realizes the truth.

Imagine the accomplishments if she started her search at home within herself.

Home

# 26 Home

The dark is the source of the light. The stillness is the beginning of movement.

The wise woman is able to travel without ever leaving her home. Even when there is much distraction, she stays centered in her self.

Why would a wise woman run about like a chicken? When you become unattached, you forget where your home is; when you let others influence you, you lose touch with yourself.

# Reflections

Journeying

56

# 27 Journeying

Even the desert holds gifts for those attempting to cross. The camel evolves as is necessary.

Plot your course. Map your journey. Lose your way in life's bends and turns. Follow the road less traveled and arrive daily at your destination.

Getting lost is a matter of perspective. Be prepared, but travel with a light load.

# Reflections

Opposites

# 28 Opposites

In the dance of life, opposites create the play.
Male is not better than female; light is not better
than darkness. Both are essential to the whole.

If you only see the differences, you lose your
perspective. Climb a mountain to see the valleys.
Both have lessons to teach.

Admiring the statue, the wise woman appreciates
the stone. Possibilities become endless when we
look to the source.

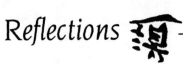 Reflections

Seasons

60

# 29 Seasons

Celebrate the changing seasons of your life:
Youth, Adolescence, Woman, Crone. Imitate
Mother Nature as if you had a choice.

All things have their time. Don't push or block
the river; it goes where it must go.

## Reflections

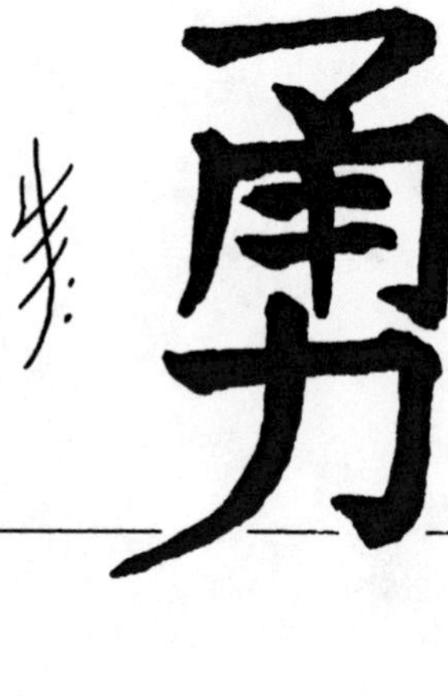

Courage

# 30 Courage

Women, venturing into the unknown, create paths for those who follow. Doing something first creates opportunities for others to do it also. It becomes less risky.

Wise women remember their grandmothers, yet also go their own way. It is the Tao of women to be explorers.

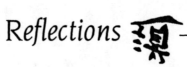 Reflections

Silence

64

# 31 Silence

Silence is the tool of oppressors. Speak out!
Who will speak our truth if not for you or me?
Speak out! If no one hears our words, who will
learn our language? Speak out! If no one learns
our language, who will understand us? Speak
out! If no one understands us, we will be
misunderstood. Speak out!

Surround yourself with women and speak your
truth. Both men and women will listen.

Who will break the silence? Speak out! Who will
teach our daughters if not for you and me?
Speak out!

Women and Men:
The Tao

# 32 Women and Men: The Tao

**M**en and women in harmony reflect the Tao.
When working together, the sum of the parts is
greater than the whole.

Man is not greater, woman is not more beautiful;
words are but reflections of the person who
speaks. The rivers run separate courses only to
merge in the ocean. The earth accepts the sun at
the end of each day.

Depending on your perspective, the sun in the
noon sky is either rising or setting.

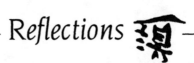

*Know Thyself*

# 33  Know Thyself

Seek the wisdom of knowing others. Stay still and know thyself. Breath in.

Work to organize your life. Stay still and see the patterns. Breath out.

Prioritize and create your goals. Stay still and see the way.

Breath in; breath out. Breath in; breath out.

Stay still. There, between your breaths, know thyself.

# Reflections

Women's Mysteries

# 34 Women's Mysteries

Light follows darkness; darkness succeeds the
light. Lunar cycles reflect only parts of the
whole; instinctual patterns echo the moon.
Trust your intuition to guide you home.

No more than the moon, no less than the sun.
Unfathomable mysteries celebrated by initiates
long ago.

*Walking the Sacred Way*

# 35  Walking the Sacred Way

There is not a path that has not already been walked by the women who have gone before. You do not walk this path alone.

Demeter, Persephone, Athena, Penelope, Diana, Deborah, Cecilia. All have been here before you. You do not walk this path alone.

Their journeys, their lives, their stories remain to guide your way. Listen to the women who have walked before you. You will not lose your way.

Reflections

The Way of Women

74

# 36 The Way of Women

She allows the daughter, sitting beside her, to take the first stitch. The wise woman does not rush in to take it apart. She smiles, acknowledges, and continues to sew her own stitches.

The daughters model the mothers. Act wisely.

The daughters are watching.

Transformation

# 37 Transformation

Do more by doing less. Life is transformed
during periods of inactivity. Do nothing, and you
will begin to know the Tao of women.

Scripts

# 38  Scripts

The wise woman plays the roles she is given
but creates her own script. She recognizes the
truth and does not try to maintain illusions.

Not limiting herself, she does not blame others.

She is free to create her own adventures.

# Reflections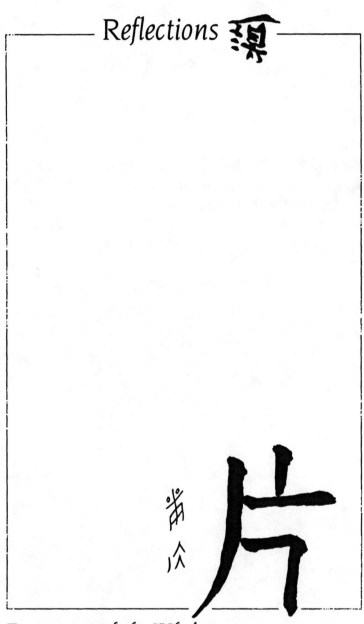

Fragments of the Whole

# 39  Fragments of the Whole

The wise woman recognizes the whole in each
small part. Nothing in life is wasted. Everything has
a part and a place.

Each snowflake in a snowstorm is unique. Each
block in a quilt is different. Together, they blanket
the earth. Apart, the pattern is lost.

The wise woman views each piece with compassion
and hope. She knows that each one contributes to
the whole. Like a master quilter, she brings
together the pieces and parts to create life around
her.

# Reflections

Return

82

# 40 Return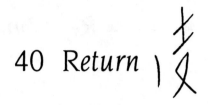

Once the dragons are faced, the deserts are crossed, and the forest path is cleared, it is time to return.

Choose wisely. Gather your gifts and remember your lessons. You are fragile now. Be gentle with yourself.

From the outside – go in. From the inside – go out. The boundaries are permeable but dangerous. Memories are claimed and lessons forgotten.

Seek out other sojourners and speak your truths, lest they be forgotten.

# Reflections

Path

# 41 Path

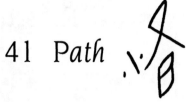

The wise woman hearing about the Tao begins
to follow its path. The ordinary woman ponders
which road to take. The foolish woman sees only
obstacles in the way.

Some say the path is dark and endless.

The wise woman continues on her journey,
creating light in the darkness and a path where
there was none.

Her footprints mark the way.

共

OK:

Community of One

# 42  Community of One

One creates two. Two create three. All things are borne of woman. Male and female working together in harmony, opposites converging, bring the possibility of true union. Possibilities are endless.

Many dislike being alone. The wise woman uses solitude to experience aloneness. Remembering her place in the scheme of things, she recognizes her connection to the entire world.

Gentle

# 43 Gentle

Women's ways are gentle and can overcome the hard. When there is flexibility, there is space for the new. There is value in gentleness.

In the blowing of the wind, the reed bends and holds its own. Growing in the dark, the moss points the way.

The wise woman, going with the flow, smoothes even the sharpest rock.

# Reflections

Contentment

# 44  Contentment

What is more important to you: being famous or being honest? What is more valued by you: being wealthy or being content? What is more difficult for you: being successful or failing?

If you look to others for your contentment, you cannot be content. If contentment depends on wealth, you will not be content with yourself.

When you are happy with things as they are, you can celebrate what you have. When you become aware that nothing is missing, your world is in harmony.

Doing the Work of the Tao

# 45 Doing the Work of the Tao

When working with the pieces, the whole may be difficult to see. The work may seem impossible, but the impossible can happen.

Daily work seems tedious, but the tasks are eventually completed.

Letting things happen naturally, the wise woman steps aside.

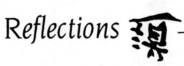

Fear

# 46 Fear

Facing the unknown, the wise woman becomes cautious. Fear does not stop her from venturing forth.

Using the energy created by fear, she transforms her visions to safety. She brings her children with her.

Creating safety, there is nothing left to fear.

Men and women live in harmony.

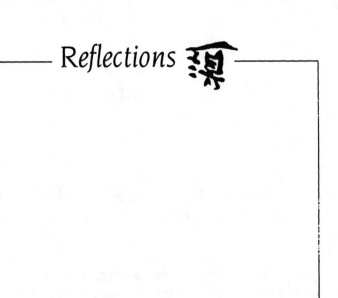

# Reflections

Trusting Emotions

96

# 47 Trusting Emotions

When you don't judge your feelings, you can experience a world of possibilities. By trusting your emotions, you can understand the Tao of women.

The more facts you gather, the harder it is to understand.

Without leaving, the wise woman begins her journey. She trusts her emotions and understands without trying.

Rituals

# 48  Rituals

When learning about the sacred, one becomes aware of the profane. Opposition is created. One becomes better than another.

When the ordinary becomes sacred, all of life is honored. Daily tasks become rituals.

The doing and the not doing are the Tao of women.

Reflections

Family

100

# 49 Family

Extending her family ties, the wise woman embraces all humanity. Acting with mothers everywhere, she creates villages to raise each child.

When the family is confused, she is blamed and works harder.

When the family is in harmony, she acknowledges their accomplishments.

She is mother to the human family.

*Rhythms of Living*

# 50  Rhythms of Living

The wise woman releases herself to the cycles and rhythms of living. She knows that all must end, and is able to let go of all things.

There are no fantasies in her mind, no vanities in her body. She doesn't contrive her behaviors; she acts from the seasons of her heart.

She does not retreat from living; she is aware of her own mortality. She knows that a rose returns to the earth after its blossoms are spent.

Mother Nature

104

# 51  Mother Nature

When seeking the Tao, look to Mother Nature.
Rivers flowing to the sea, trees turning with the
seasons, the earth bringing forth food, the cactus
blooming in the desert.

The wise woman instinctively clings to her roots.
Following Mother Nature is the Tao of women.
Understanding is in the way things are.

Reflections 源

# Reflections 源

尋

Finding Your Way

# 52 Finding Your Way

The Tao is the beginning. Everything has come from it; everything will return to it.

To find your way, go back to the beginning. You must go back the way you came.

When you see the children, follow them to the parents. Your grief will be lifted when you remember where you came from.

When you see through the darkness, there is light. When you retreat, you are strong. Look inside and find your own way.

Life is not always as it seems. Refrain from making judgments and being misled by appearances.

You are on the right path.

Staying on the Path
When the Way is Lost

108

# 53  Staying on the Path
## When the Way is Lost

If the way is lost, remain quiet until you find it.
There is something inside you that knows in
which direction to go.

If the road is wide, walk side by side. When the
road narrows, walk alone. The bridges you cross
were built by someone who knows the way.

When many are wealthy while others go hungry,
and resources are spent on bombs instead of
babies, the path becomes lost and the way
forgotten.

Stay still and remember. In the stillness, you will
find your way.

# Reflections

Women Who Have Gone Before

# 54 Women Who Have Gone Before

Women who live with the Tao will not be forgotten. Women who walk with the Tao will not become lost. Their names will be remembered as those who have gone before.

When you bring the Tao to your living, you become who you were meant to be. When the Tao is present in your family, your family will be nourished. When the Tao is present where you live, your geography will become a place that teaches other places on the planet. When the Tao is present in the world, a global song may be heard.

How can this be true? Look inside yourself. Listen to those who have gone before. Listen to your voice as it speaks your mother's words. Women who have gone before are not forgotten.

Natural Immunity

# 55  Natural Immunity

She who lives her life with the Tao is like a young sapling. The trunk is flexible, the bark is tender, but its roots are firmly in the earth. It doesn't know about how babies are conceived, yet it carries within it new life. It can bend in the winds forever and not be blown over because it is in harmony with the earth.

Wise women have natural immunity. They let everything ebb and flow, without work, without desiring. They let go of expectations and they are never at a loss. Because they are not at a loss, their spirits live forever.

Creative Spirit

# 56  Creative Spirit

 X

 开

The muse's energy is tapped when you stop and listen to the silence inside. Creating sparks of brilliance from barely glowing embers, she is only a breath away.

Expressions of the self wait to be birthed. Look to the potter's hand, the weaver's eye, the basket maker's techniques.

The creative spirit lives on in women's tasks.

Ordinary to Heroic

# 57 Ordinary to Heroic

If you care about men and women, become aware of the Tao. When you stop trying and loosen your grip on others, life takes care of itself.

The more rules you make, the less people will follow them. The more objects you have, the less safe you will feel. The more you take care of others, the less people will take of themselves.

The wise woman says, "I forget the rules, and people follow their own. I do not control the purse strings and people make their own money. I do not preach religion and people become more spiritual. I forget about making everyone good and people become good on their own."

The heroic woman, conducting her life in ordinary fashion, achieves the extraordinary.

Generations of women teaching children, growing food, making clothing, creating homes.

What could be more heroic?

Giving Yourself Away

# 57 Giving Yourself Away

When women are treated with respect, all people are respected. When women are oppressed, all people become repressed and dishonest.

When the people who hold the power have high expectations, inferior results occur. When you try to cheer people up, you prepare them for discontent. When you try to make people honest, you prepare the foundation for dishonesty.

The wise woman is happy to be a model and not to try to control others. She is sharp but does not stab others. She is direct but with humility. She shines brightly, but does not blind others.

Above all, respect yourself. Give your time, your energy, your money, but not your soul.

When you live for another person, you have no life of your own. When you give yourself away, there is nothing left.

Who will respect those who do not respect themselves?

Nurturing

120

# 59 Nurturing

Nurturing is important for leadership. Guiding requires compassion. Patience is valued and permeates everything. Resolve and commitment are solid, yet flexible.

A bird instinctively feeds her young. Everything is possible.

# Reflections

Incubation

# 60 Incubation

A wise woman knows that to bake a good souffle she cannot open the oven door too soon nor jar the contents unnecessarily.

Give yourself the time and space to grow to your full potential. As your power grows, evil cannot harm you. You've learned how to step around it.

Do not become a victim and the oppression will stop.

Receptive

# 61 Receptive

Streams and rivers are welcomed into the ocean. Accepting everyone, no one is left out. When one knows she is a part of something larger than herself, she can relax.

The river floods when its banks are full. Respect your limits; just do what you can do.

Telling the Stories

126

# 62 Telling the Stories

Women's ways are central to the world. Wise women value them; foolish people shun them.

Awards can be secured by exceptional work; honor can be achieved by excelling; however, women's ways are beyond reward and cannot be bought or earned.

When an extraordinary woman is found, sit by her side. Watch and listen as she weaves her stories into your life.

Why do we value our elders? Because they hold the stories that connect our families.

Discrimination:
Sorting Seeds

# 63 Discrimination:
## Sorting Seeds

Be without doing; work without strain. Think of the individual as universal and all women as family. Confront the difficult while it is still easy. Complete large tasks through a number of small actions.

The wise woman does not expect greatness. She becomes great when adversity presents itself. She attends to the details and the problem is resolved.

Beginnings Without Ends

# 64  Beginnings Without Ends

What has already begun is simple to nurture. What is new is easy to change. What is rigid can be easily broken. What is loose can be dislodged.

Prevention is easiest before the difficulty begins. Planning for order comes before the beginning. The oak tree grows from an acorn. A long journey begins with a single step.

When beginnings are rushed, failures result. Trying to control, control is lost. Forcing an ending destroys the natural completion.

The wise woman acts by participating in the unfolding. She remains serene in the process.

Simple Patterns

# 65 Simple Patterns

Wise women do not try to change people, but provide an example of survival. When people think they know the right way, they are difficult to change. When people understand that they do not know, they then can begin to change.

If you want to learn about women, do not try to control or direct them. The ordinary way is the most simple. When you are at peace with the obvious, you can help people find their way to their authentic selves.

Reflections

Collaborating

# 66 Collaborating

Working in harmony with others, the wise woman is able to accomplish great things. This has always been the way of women. Sewing quilts, making baskets, growing food, the community is one family.

Isolation has not proven healthy, for the individual or for the community. It is better to remember the old ways.

Gifts to Herself

# 67 Gifts to Herself

Moving through life the wise woman faces three tasks: learning to know herself, learning to trust herself, and learning to take risks.

Knowing herself, she learns to know others. Trusting herself, she learns she can trust others. Taking risks, she gains the courage to let go.

The wise woman receives the best gifts from herself.

# Reflections

玩

*Playful Spirit*

# 68  Playful Spirit

Children playing make up the rules as they go;
they color outside the lines and create imaginary
playmates.

The imaginary becomes real. The real is imaginary.
There are no boundaries.

Patience

140

# 69  Patience

When planting a seed the gardener does not
expect immediate results. There is much to be
done in preparation for the growth.

Moving forward often requires stepping back.
Yielding, the wise woman gains ground.

渠

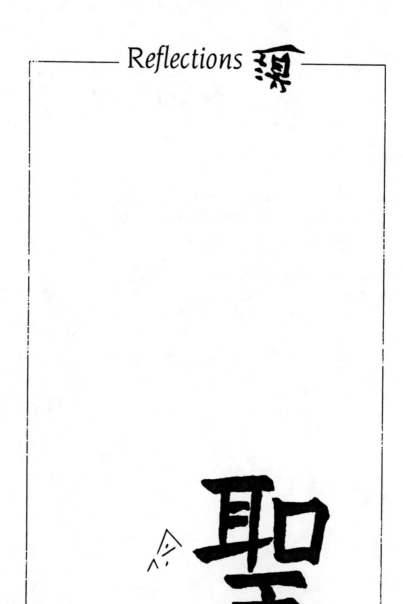

Spirituality

# 70 Spirituality

Women's ways are of the spirit and of the earth. How can this be understood?

Feeling her beliefs and acting on her intuition, the wise woman honors the connections she has been given.

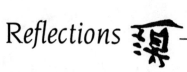

Healing

144

# 71 Healing

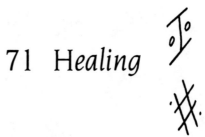

Being empty creates opportunity for growth. Is the womb a place of emptiness?

When a woman accepts her problems, she is ready to begin her healing.

Crisis is an opportunity. The wise woman perceives the truth and is prepared for becoming whole. The healing occurs after the wounding.

Modeling

# 72  Modeling

When people forget their wisdom, they seek
leaders. When they do not trust their wisdom, they
depend on messengers.

The knowing woman distances herself so there will
be no misunderstandings. She models the message
so others can discover their own wisdom.

# Reflections

Web of the World

# 73 Web of the World

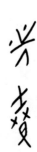

Women of the Tao are at peace. They survive without competing, speak without words, know when to leave, and live without controlling.

The Tao is the web of the world. Though there is space between the strands, nothing falls through the web.

Capturing what is needed, holding tightly, and letting go lightly. Connections.

The Tao of women.

# Reflections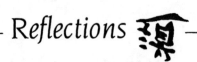

Change

150

# 74  Change

When women know that everything changes,
they are free to let go. If there is no fear of loss,
everything is possible.

When you try to prevent change, it is like trying
to be the creator. Playing the role of creator
increases the risk of loss.

# Reflections

Cutting the Cord

152

# 75  Cutting the Cord

When the price is too great, people go without.
When the country is too repressive, women lose
their freedom.

When people work together, they can create
possibility.

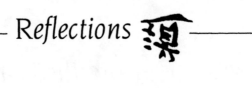

# Reflections

*Subtleties*

# 76 Subtleties

Women survive by being flexible; rigid, they become brittle and break.

Whatever is resilient adapts to the environment. Whatever is unyielding and forceful foretells of failure and death.

Women who are pliant and subtle maintain a way of life. The rigid and difficult will not survive. The flexible and gentle will continue.

Stability

156

# 77 Stability

In the world, the Tao is like a dance. The music provides a balance to the movement of the dance. Both are needed to create stability.

Those who try to alter the balance to protect their power go against the Tao. They move too fast and do not listen to the music. Power shifts the natural order.

The wise woman continues to dance because there is no end to her music. She moves without thinking, continues without fatigue, and values the contributions of others.

With nature providing the balance, harmony is created. Firmly rooted to the earth, the wise woman is free to move to the beat of her own music.

# Reflections 淇

Power of the Feminine

# 78 Power of the Feminine

Water yields, yet it is able to wear down rocks and stone. The gentle wears out the hard. The easy outlasts the difficult. All people know this to be true, yet few practice gentleness.

The wise woman, therefore, continues in the face of difficulty. Because she has given up supporting, she becomes others' greatest support.

The power of the feminine is paradoxical.

# Reflections

Self-Responsibility

# 79  Self-Responsibility

Taking responsibility for her life, the wise woman is not content with being a victim; she moves beyond her wounds and tells a different story.

Getting stuck in the blaming does not end the victimization. Life may be unfair to those who do not realize the possibility for growth.

Setting Priorities: Saying No

162

# 80 Setting Priorities: Saying No

Try to ford a rushing stream weighted down by the mantles of societal expectations and you will drown.

The wise woman learns to say "no" so the children can do for themselves. This, she knows, is healthy. Doing for others creates dependency and resentment.

## Reflections 漠

Knowing Women

164

# 81 Knowing Women

**K**nowing women return to greet the women who follow. Wise women rest, knowing that freedom comes from the journey itself.

The Tao of women nourishes; the path is well tended.

# Bibliography

Aburdene, P. and J. Naisbitt. *Megatrends for Women*. New York: Villard Books, 1992.

Allen, Paula Gunn. *Spider Woman's Granddaughters: Traditional Tales and Contemporary Writing by Native American Women*. New York: Ballantine Books, 1989.

Anderson, Sherry Ruth and Patricia Hopkins. *The Feminine Face of God, the Unfolding of the Sacred in Women*. New York: Bantam Books, 1991.

Armstrong, Christopher. *Evelyn Underhill: An Introduction to Her Life and Writings*. Oxford: A.B. Mowbray & Co. Ltd., 1975.

Barber, Elizabeth Wayland. *Women's Work: The First 20,000 Years*. New York: W.W. Norton & Co., 1994.

Bateson, Mary Catherine. *Composing a Life*. New York: A Plume Book, Penguin Group, 1989.

Bateson, Mary Catherine. *Peripheral Visions*. New York: Harper Collins, 1994.

Belenky, M., et al. *Women's Ways of Knowing: the Development of Self, Voice and Mind*. New York: Basic Books, Harper Collins, 1986.

Bolen, Jean Shinoda. *Crossing to Avalon*. San Francisco: Harper, 1994.

Bolen, Jean Shinoda. *Goddesses in Everywoman: Psychology of Women*. San Francisco: Harper and Row, 1984.

Bolen, Jean Shinoda. *The Tao of Psychology*. New York: Harper & Row Publishers Inc., 1979.

Boulding, E. *The Underside of History*. Boulder, Colorado: Westview Press Inc., 1976.

Brennan, S. and J. Winklepeck. *Resourceful Woman*. Detroit, Michigan: Visible Inc., 1994.

Brown, R.M. *Starting from Scratch*. New York: Bantam Books, 1988.

Brown, Lyn Mikel and Carol Gilligan. *Meeting at the Crossroads: Women's Psychology and Girl's Development*. New York: Ballantine Books, 1992.

Bruchae, Carol, Linda Hogan and Judith McDaniel. *The Stories We Hold Secret: Tales of Women's Spiritual Development*. Greenfield City, New York: Greenfield Review Press, 1986.

Bukovinsky, Janet. *Women of Words: A Personal Introduction to Thirty-five Important Writers*. Philadelphia: Running Press, 1994.

Cameron, Anne. *Daughters of Copper Woman*. Vancouver, British Columbia: Publishers, 1981.

Campbell, Joseph. *The Hero with a Thousand Faces*. Princeton: Princeton University Press, 1949.

Campbell, Joseph and Charles Muses. *In All Her Names, Explorations of the Feminine in Divinity*. San Francisco: Harper, 1991.

Capra, F. *The Tao of Physics*. New York: Bantam Books, 1975.

Carter, Angela. *The Old Wives Fairy Tale Book*. New York: Pantheon Fairy Tale & Folklore Library, 1990.

Chesler, Phyllis. *Women and Madness*. New York: Avon, a Division of Hearst Corp., 1972.

Chernin, Kim. *Reinventing Eve: Modern Woman in Search of Herself*. New York: Times Books, Random House, 1987.

Christ, Carol P. *Diving Deep and Surfacing: Women on Spiritual Quest*. Boston: Beacon Press, 1980.

Conway, Jill Ker. *True North*. New York: Alfred A. Knopf, 1994.

Cooper, Patricia and Allen, and Norma Bradley. *The Quilters: Women and Domestic Art, an Oral History*. New York: An Anchor Book, Doubleday & Company Inc., 1989.

Dalton, Jerry O. *The Tao Te Ching: Backward Down the Path*. Atlanta, Georgia: Humanics New Age, 1994.

de Balza, Honore. *Seraphita*. New York: Steiner Books, 1976.

de Castillejo, Irene Claremont. *Knowing Woman: A Feminine Psychology*. New York: Harper Colophon Books, 1973.

Dillard, A. *The Writing Life*. New York: Harper & Row Publishers, 1989.

Dreher, D. *The Tao of Peace*. New York: Donald I. Fine Inc., 1990.

Duerk, Judith. *Circle of Stones: Woman's Journey to Herself*. San Diego: Luramedia, 1989.

Duncan, Isadora. *My Life*. New York: Garden City Publishing Co., 1927.

Edgerly, Lois Stiles. *Women's Words, Women's Stories, An American Daybook*. Gardiner, Maine: Tilbury House, 1994.

Eliade, Mircea. *Rites and Symbols of Initiation: The Mysteries of Birth and Rebirth*. New York: Harper Torchbooks, 1958.

Feng, G. and J. English. *Lao Tsu: Tao te Ching*. New York: Alfred A. Knopf Inc., 1972.

Fields, R. et al. *Chop Wood, Carry Water*. Los Angeles: Jeremy P. Tarcher Inc., 1984.

Fierz, David and Linda. *Women's Dionysian Initiation: The Villa of Mysteries in Pompeii*. Dallas: Spring Publications, 1988.

Flagg, Fannie. *Fried Green Tomatoes at the Whistle Stop Cafe*. New York: McGraw-Hill Book Co., 1987.

French, David J. *In Search of the Real Me: Achieving Personal Balance*. Atlanta, Georgia: Humanics New Age, 1992.

Gilligan, Carol. *In a Different Voice*. Cambridge, Massachusetts: Harvard University Press, 1982.

Goldberg, N. *Long Quiet Highway*. New York: Bantam Books, 1993.

Goldberg, N. *Wild Mind*. New York: Bantam Books, 1990.

Goldberg, N. *Writing Down the Bones*. Boston: Shambhala, 1986.

Grigg, Ray. *The Tao of Being: A Think and Do Workbook*. Atlanta, Georgia: Humanics New Age, 1994.

Grigg, Ray. *The Tao of Relationships: A Balancing of Man and Woman*. Atlanta, Georgia: Humanics New Age, 1988.

Haggard, H. Rider. *She*. Amsterdam: Quick Fox, 1981.

Hall, Nor. *The Moon and the Virgin – Reflections on the Archetypal Feminine*. New York: Harper and Row Publishers, 1980.

Hall, Nor. *Mothers and Daughters*. Minneapolis: Rusoff Books, 1976.

Harding, M. Esther. *Woman's Mysteries Ancient and Modern*. New York: G.P. Putnam's Sons, 1971.

Heider, John. *The Tao of Leadership*. Atlanta, Georgia: Humanics New Age, 1986.

Heilbrun, Carolyn G. *Hamlet's Mother an Other Women*. New York: Ballantine Books, 1990.

Heilbrun, Carolyn G. *Writing a Woman's Life*. New York: Ballantine Books, 1988.

Hillman, James. *Facing the Gods*. Dallas: Spring Publications, 1980.

Hurston, Zora Neale. *Their Eyes Were Watching God*. New York: Perennial Library, Harper Row, 1973.

James, E.O. *The Cult of the Mother Goddess: An Archeological and Documentary Study*. New York: Frederick A Praeger Publishers, 1959.

Johnson, Robert A. *She: Understanding Feminine Psychology*. Religious Publishing Co., 1976.

Jung, C.G. and C. Kereny. *Essays on a Science of Mythology: The Myth of the Divine Child and the Mysteries of Eleusis*. Princeton: Princeton University Press, 1969.

Keen, Sam and Anne Valley-Fox. *Your Mythic Journey: Finding Meaning in Your Life Through Writing and Storytelling*. Los Angeles: Jeremy Tarcher, 1973.

Kerenyi, Karl. *Goddesses of Sun and Moon*. Dallas: Spring Publications, 1979.

Kerenyi, Karl. *Eleusis: Archetypal Image of Mother and Daughter*. New York: Schocken Books, 1977.

170

Kingston, Maxine Hong. *The Woman Warrior: Memoirs of a Childhood Among Ghosts*. New York: Vintage International - Vintage Books, 1989.

Koller, Alice. *An Unknown Woman, A Journey of Self-discovery*. New York: Bantam Books, 1981.

Koppelman, Susan. *Women's Friendships: A Collection of Short Stories*. Norman: University of Oklahoma Press, 1991.

Leary, Lewis. *Kate Chopin: The Awakening and Other Stories*. New York: Holt, Rinehart & Winston Inc., 1970.

Leary, Timothy. *Psychedelic Prayers: After the Tao te Ching*. Kerkonkson, New York: Poets Press, 1966.

Leguin, Ursula K. *Dancing at the Edge of the World*. New York: Grove Press, 1989.

Lessing, Doris. *The Golden Notebook*. New York: Bantam Books, Simon & Shuster, 1962.

Levertov, Denise. *Breathing the Water*. New York: A New Directions Book, 1984.

Lifshin, Lyn. *Ariadne's Thread, A Collection of Contemporary Women's Journals*. New York: Harper Colophon, 1982.

Lindbergh, Anne Morrow. *Gift from the Sea*. New York: Vintage Books, Random House, 1955.

Lowinsky, Naomi Ruth. *Stories from the Motherline, Reclaiming the Mother-Daughter Bond, Finding Our Feminine Souls*. Los Angeles: Jeremy P. Tarcher, 1992.

Luke, Helen. *Kaleidoscope: The Way of Woman & Other Essays*. New York: Parabola Books, 1992.

Mairs, Nancy. *Remembering the Bone House*. New York: Perennial Library, Harper & Row, 1989.

Metz, Pamela. *The Tao of Learning*. Atlanta, Georgia, Humanics New Age, 1994.

Middleton, Ruth. *Alexandra David-Neel: Portrait of an Adventurer*. Boston: Shambhala Publications, 1989.

Mitchell, S. *Tao te Ching*. New York: Harper & Row Publishers Inc., 1988.

Moon, Sheila. *Changing Woman & Her Sisters*. San Francisco: Guild for Psychological Studies Publishing House, 1984.

Moore, Rickie. *A Goddess in My Shoes: Seven Steps to Peace*. Atlanta, Georgia: Humanics New Age, 1988.

Murdock, Maureen. *The Heroine's Journey: Woman's Quest for Wholeness*. Boston: Shambhala, 1990.

Nelson, Gertrude Mueller. *Here All Dwelt Free: Stories to Heal the Wounded Feminine*. New York: Doubleday & Company Inc., 1991.

Newman, Molly and Barbara Damashek. *Quilters: A Play*. New York: Dramatists Play Service Inc., 1986.

Niethammer, Carolyn. *Daughters of the Earth: The Lives & Legends of American Indian Women*. New York: Collier Books, Macmillan, 1977.

Oakes, Maud. *The Stone Speaks: The Memoir of a Personal Transformation*. Wilmette, Illinois: Chiron Publications, 1987.

Oliver, Mary. *New and Selected Poems*. Boston: Beacon Press, 1992.

Olsen, Tillie. *Silences*. New York: Delta Seymour Lawrence, Dell Publishing, 1965.

Pearson, Carol and Katherine Pope. *The Female Hero in American and British Literature*. New York: R.R. Bowker Co., 1981.

Pijoan, Teresa. *White Wolf Woman and Other Native American Transformation Myths*. Little Rock: August House Publishers Inc., 1992.

Plaskow, Judith and Carol P. Christ. *Weaving the Visions: New Patterns in Feminist Spirituality*. San Francisco: Harper, 1989.

172

Pomeroy, Sarah B. *Goddesses, Whores, Wives and Slaves: Women in Classical Antiquity*. New York: Schocken Books, 1975.

Rose, Phyllis (ed.). *The Norton Book of Women's Lives*. New York: Norton & Co., 1993.

Russell, Willy. *Shirley Valentine*. New York: Samuel French Inc., 1988.

Sarton, May. *Journal of a Solitude*. New York: Norton & Co., 1973.

Schreiner, Olive. *Dreams*. Pacific Grove, California: Select Books, 1971.

Scott-Maxwell, F. *The Measure of My Days*. New York: Alfred A. Knopf, 1968.

Sewell, Marilyn. *Cries of the Spirit: A Celebration of Women's Spirituality*. Boston: Beacon Press, 1991.

Shange, Ntozake. *For Colored Girls Who Have Considered Suicide When the Rainbow is Enuf*. New York: Collier Books, Macmillan Publishing, 1975.

Simpkinson, Charles and Anne. *Sacred Stories: A Celebration of the Power of Stories to Transform and Heal*. San Francisco: Harper, 1993.

Sojourner, Mary. *Sisters of the Dream*. Arizona: Northland Publishing, 1989.

Stein, D. *The Kwan Yin Book of Changes*. St Paul, Minnesota: Llewellyn Publications, 1985.

Ulanov, Ann Belford. *The Feminine*. Evanston: Northwestern University Press, 1971.

Ulanov, Ann Belford. *Receiving Woman: Studies in the Psychology and Theology of the Feminine*. Philadelphia: Westminster Press, 1981.

Ullman, Liv. *Changing*. New York: Alfred A. Knopf, 1977.

Walker, Alice. *In Search of Mother's Garden*. Harvest/HBJ Books, Harcourt Brace Jovanovich Publishers, 1983.

Walker, B. *The Woman's Dictionary of Symbols and Sacred Objects*. San Francisco: Harper & Row, 1988.

Wall, Steve. *Wisdom's Daughters: Conversations with Women Elders of Native America*. New York: Harper Collins, 1993.

Waters, Frank. *The Woman at Otowi Crossing*. Athens: Swallow Press, Ohio University Press, 1987.

Wheelwright, Jane Hollister. *The Death of a Woman: How a Life Became Complete*. New York: St Martin's Press, 1981.

Whyte, David. *Where Many Rivers Meet*. Langley, Washington: Many Rivers Press, 1993.

Whyte, David. *Fire in the Earth*. Langley, Washington: Many Rivers Press, 1992.

Wolkstein, Diane and Samuel Noah Kramer. *Inanna – Queen of Heaven and Earth: Her Stories and Hymns from Sumer*. New York: Harper Colophon Books, 1983.

Woolf, Virginia. *A Room of One's Own*. Troy, New Jersey: Harvest/HBJ Books, Harcourt Brace Jovanovich Publishers, 1929.

Wing, R.L. *The Illustrated I Ching*. New York: Doubleday & Company Inc., 1982.

Wing, R.L. *The Tao of Power*. New York: Doubleday & Company Inc., 1986.

# About the Authors

Pamela Metz lives in Denver, Colorado where she is the associate dean of the University of Denver Graduate School of Social Work. She holds degrees in education and social work from Illinois State University, The University of Denver, and The University of Colorado. A teacher of a vast array of subjects, her thirty year career spans university settings, public and private schools, and the innovative University Without Walls. She has worked as an elementary teacher, hospice social worker, and educational administrator. On all these paths, the wisdom of the Tao has been her guide: letting go, following natural cycles, trusting the processes.

Jacqueline Tobin also lives in Denver, Colorado with her husband and two adopted children. She teaches a course on women's stories in the Women's Studies Department at The University of Denver, and holds degrees in education, women's studies, and counseling. As a freelance writer she travels around the country collecting women's personal narratives; she is the creator of "Storylines," an educational counseling program developed to gather and preserve women's life histories. She has worked as a therapist, educator, writer, and mother. In all these endeavors she sees herself as a student and facilitator of the ways of women.

# About the Artists

Shi-huei Cheng learned Nu Shu by doing extensive fieldwork in Hunan Province with the few surviving women who still used Nu Shu and by editing some of the original manuscripts and their Mandarin translations. She was instrumental in putting the original Nu Shu into a book published by the Awakening Press (Taiwan) in 1991. Ms Cheng has served as the Editor-in-Chief of Awakening Press and Awakening Magazine, and is a board member of the Awakening Foundation. Currently she is the Editor-in-Chief of the bimonthly Eslite Book Review in Taiwan.

The traditional Chinese calligraphy for The Tao of Women was created by Mr. Lian Xaiochuan. A native of Wuhan city, in Hubei province China, he currently resides in New York City.

# Reflections

Both authors of The Tao of Women have worked extensively with women's studies and women's issues. Pamela, as an educator and administrator, has counseled many women along their paths. Jacqueline, as a freelance writer, collects women's stories. Traveling the country in search of personal narratives, she finds and records women's lives.

The authors are interested, not only in your reactions to the book, but also in your stories and wisdom. If you would like to assist in their search for women's stories and insights, please send your favorite reflection to:

Humanics Limited
Reflections
PO Drawer 77766
Atlanta, GA 30357

It is preferred that your reflection be typewritten and no longer than one page. Be sure to include your name, address, and telephone number. The authors will not be able to acknowledge each individual reflection. By sending your reflection, you are granting the authors permission to include part or all of your correspondence in their work, or in any subsequent editions of The Tao of Women. Please be sure to specify if you would like your name, or any other information held in confidence.

LaVergne, TN USA
04 February 2010
172119LV00004B/63/A

9 780893 342371